Age-Proof Your Brain!

Brain Games To Go is a trademark of Publications International, Ltd.

© 2010 Publications International, Ltd.

ISBN-13: 978-1-60553-011-6
ISBN-10: 1-60553-011-5

Manufactured in China.

8 7 6 5 4 3 2 1

TV Westerns

Terms in the grid are all titles of classic TV westerns. Words can be found horizontally, vertically, or diagonally. They may read either backward or forward. The leftover letters reveal the names of a popular TV western's stars.

BEST OF THE WEST

BIG VALLEY (The)

BONANZA

BRONCO

CHEYENNE

CIMARRON CITY

CISCO KID (The)

DEPUTY (The)

GUNSMOKE

KUNG FU

LARAMIE

MAVERICK

RAWHIDE

REBEL (The)

RIFLEMAN (The)

SHENANDOAH (A Man Called)

SUGARFOOT

TATE

TRACKDOWN

VIRGINIAN (The)

WAGON TRAIN

WELLS FARGO

YANCY DERRINGER

ZORRO (The Mask of)

HIDDEN MESSAGE: _____

_____

```
H A O D N A N E H S L E B E R
D O G R A F S L L E W A N R B
L T O C M A V E R I C K E K B
E K O E E K O M S N U G U R E
L I O O L R N E B G N N R E S
C E M N F N A I N I G R I V T
E I M A I R G I R F C C H A O
D E S L R V A R U H L T A N F
E E D C A A E G E O N A A B T
P N D L O D L Y U D P E R T H
U Z L I Y K E R N S E O L L E
T E O C H N I A R T N O G A W
Y R N R N W O D K C A R T O E
B A E E R R A B O N A N Z A S
Y T I C N O R R A M I C T S T
```

Answers on page 28.

British Universities

Every word listed below is contained within this group of letters. Words can be found horizontally, vertically, or diagonally. They may read either backward or forward.

```
L O T S I R B R E A D I N G K
E L L O E E E G D I R B M A C
E D O T S T I R L I N G H M I
D L S U E S L X E S S E E A W
N L E X G E O X F O R D R H R
U K E E E H E N U I T O I G A
D E E D K C B T R A S T O N W
G C S N H N H O P E N P T I O
S A I N T A N D R E W S W M G
Q U O T M M S T N O G I A R S
U K S P Y E R R U S U H T I A
E R T S L E N U R B R G T B L
E O L A E D I N B U R G H L G
N Y W E N X N O D N O L U D E
S T R A T H C L Y D E H T A B
```

ASTON	GLASGOW	READING
BATH	HERIOT-WATT	SAINT ANDREWS
BIRMINGHAM	HULL	SOUTHAMPTON
BRISTOL	KEELE	STIRLING
BRUNEL	KENT	STRATHCLYDE
CAMBRIDGE	LEEDS	SURREY
CITY	LONDON	SUSSEX
DUNDEE	LOUGHBOROUGH	ULSTER
DURHAM	MANCHESTER	WALES
EDINBURGH	OPEN	WARWICK
ESSEX	OXFORD	YORK
EXETER	QUEENS	

Answers on page 28.

Sandwich Stuff

Terms in the grid are all related to this lunchtime favorite. Words can be found horizontally, vertically, or diagonally. They may read either backward or forward. The leftover letters reveal the name of a popular sandwich.

```
        O R C P
      N E H Y M E
      I U I A S E A
    O B C N T A E K P
  N E K O T S U U S R S
  N E D A L A S G G E U R
  N O N T A O A B T B E T O
  U T C I S T G T U E O H R L
    A A D N E N N M A H C D L
      B R R O A S T B E E F
      L A T F J E R T B
        O S I L Y T R
        L X S E U E
        Y H C A
        E D
```

BACON	LETTUCE	SARDINE
BOLOGNA	LOX	SAUSAGE
BREAD	ONION	SPAM
BUN	REUBEN	TOAST
CHEESE	ROAST BEEF	TOMATO
CHICKEN	ROLL	TUNA FISH
EGG SALAD	RYE	TURKEY
HAM	SALT	

HIDDEN MESSAGE: _____

Answers on page 28.

Body of Evidence

Every word listed below is contained within this group of letters. Words can be found diagonally. They may read either backward or forward.

```
        I D I B O E R K M S
      D A N U D L P C I P O T
    K H E L E B K A O A A R F I
    G U N L E O F B N I O R H R E S
  O F S S U W P Y O N O E R P A E E C
  H M E A R C M S I O D C G M K Y I N
  G Y R O O F K N K L T E K D O E B F
  E T O G F N T L U C L T N H D U B E
  F M O O N H Y O E A E A H E E E T S
  R I T E E I H O E U H N E E N A B H
  E E N N T S T K U A N P K D B M D K
  G J E G D H A S D R T D A A U I R S
  N C A L E H E N I H T N E H E E L C
  K E O C S R E L R W E O T R J R T L
    C O P K L F O I A T L E E A R B
      T S O L A O R N L M E S F T
        H E T E H O A E N R U M
        A N B G O D K D Y A
```

ALL THUMBS	DEEP THROAT	KNUCKLE UNDER
ARM-TWISTING	ELBOW ROOM	LEND A HAND
BEND AN EAR	FINGER FOOD	ON YOUR TOES
BREAK-NECK	FOOT THE BILL	PAIN IN THE
SPEED	GET OFF MY BACK	NECK
BULL'S EYE	JACKLEG	POOR-MOUTH
BY A HAIR	KNEE-JERK	SHAKE A LEG
COLD SHOULDER	KNOCK HEADS	TOE THE LINE

Answers on page 28.

6

Whatever the Weather

Every word listed below is contained within this group of letters. Words can be found horizontally, vertically, or diagonally. They may read either backward or forward.

```
C Y W D O W N P O U R I S I N
Y G N I L Z Z I R D O M I C O
C G A S N S E I K S R A E L C
L O D S D D F O L O S Y E O R
O F L I T I Y R T O L D F U E
N E I G R O M S O A E R A D H
E N A C I R R U H S E A I Y T
C L H S U E O M H N T Z R E A
E L O U D D U T Y B U Z A R E
T O R N A D O W A R N I N G W
B L U S T E R Y G Y O L D R L
S H S H O W E R N D E B W A U
T E C I D N A W O N S T A I O
S U N N Y C H I L L Y I R N F
S O V E R C A S T B A L M Y R
```

BALMY

BLIZZARD

BLUSTERY

CHILLY

CLEAR SKIES

CLOUDY

CYCLONE

DOWNPOUR

DRIZZLING

FAIR AND
    WARM

FOGGY

FOUL WEATHER

FROST

GALE

HAIL

HUMID

HURRICANE

OVERCAST

RAINY

SHOWER

SLEET

SNOW AND ICE

STORMY

SUNNY

SUNSHINE

THUNDERSTORMS

TORNADO
    WARNING

TORRID

WINDY

Answers on page 29.

On the Mountaintop

Terms in the grid are all related to mountains. Words can be found horizontally, vertically, or diagonally. They may read either backward or forward.

ADIRONDACKS	GUIDE	RIDGE
ALPS	HEIGHTS	ROCKS
ANDES	HIMALAYAS	SIERRA
APENNINES	ICE	SKIING
APPALACHIANS	INDIA	SNOW
ARARAT	LODGE	STEEP
CLIFF	MATTERHORN	SUGARLOAF
CLIMBER	NEPAL	SUMMIT
COLD	PASS	TIBET
CORDILLERA	PEAK	TOBOGGAN
CRAG	PINE	TRAIL
EVEREST	PLATEAU	URALS
FIR	PRECIPICE	VAIL
FUNICULAR	PYRENEES	VALLEY
GLACIER	RANGE	VOLCANO

```
                    E
                  C D U
                I R R L S
              G A E S O
            V L H A B M C
            S A P I A M T
          E N C I T M A I T
          D V I T L R A A L
        E U A E T A L P L I C
      S G H R R R O C K S A D E
      C D H L A P E N A K R Y N
    F A O L R A G U S S C T B A I
    O R L R V T I B E T A S P G S
  M N I V O D N S E A G D E N G B S
  C R A L U C I N U F L N L E O S K
A G L C R K P E L R M N O A N B W I O
A L A I A R R E I L I M R C R O F I R
R E N P E F Y E D E N E D I U G T E N I P
C Y O W P S P F G I E T M R D T H E I G H T S
P R E C I P I C E A S S N S N A I H C A L A P P A
```

Answers on page 29.

How About a Nice Bowl of Soup?

Every word listed below is contained within this group of letters. Words can be found horizontally, vertically, or diagonally. They may read either backward or forward.

BARLEY

BISQUE

BROTH

CHICKEN

CONSOMME

DUCK

EGG DROP

MINESTRONE

MUSHROOM

NAVY BEAN

NOODLE

ONION

POTATO

RICE

SPLIT PEA

TOMATO

TURKEY

VEGETABLE

WONTON

Answers on page 29.

Islands

Terms in the grid are all names of islands. Words can be found horizontally, vertically, or diagonally. They may read either backward or forward. The leftover letters reveal the name of a large island.

```
                              N
                           P  N
                        E  W  A
                     M  Z  F  W  Y
                     O  A  A  G  I  S
          G  N       C  R  D  N  L  A  O
          N  U  O  C    T  O  O  N  B  T  G
          O  A  A  Z  R    A  K  K  R  N  A  Y  A
          L  Y  N  I  U  E  C  I  G  D    S  L  L  P
          L  A  E  I  N  L  T  N  A  M       I  I  A
             N  A  I  O  E                   C  L  A
             K  H  D  N                       I  A
             R  D  R                          S  G
             A  O  M  A  S
             E  Y  K  S
```

ALAND	HONG KONG	SAMOA
ALCATRAZ	LONG	SARDINIA
BALI	LUZON	SICILY
CORSICA	MALTA	SKYE
CRETE	MAN	TAIWAN
GALAPAGOS	OKI	YAP
HAINAN	ORKNEY	

HIDDEN MESSAGE: _____

_____

Answers on page 29.

Money, Money, Money

Terms in the grid are all related to cash. Words can be found horizontally, vertically, or diagonally. They may read either backward or forward. The leftover letters spell a famous saying about money.

BRASS	GREENBACKS
BREAD	KRONE
CARTWHEEL	LIRE
CENT	MARK
C-NOTE	NGWEE
COIN	PENNY
CROWN	PESO
DIME	POUND
DINAR	QUARTER
DOLLAR	QUID
DOUBLE EAGLE	RAND
DOUBLOON	RIYAL
FARTHING	RUBLE
FIVE SPOT	RUPEE
FLORIN	SAWBUCK
FRANC	TWO BITS
GRAND	

HIDDEN MESSAGE: _____

_____

```
        R  A  N  D  I  M  E
      U  G  N  I  H  T  R  A  F
    B  R  T  R  H  E  Q  L  O  R  V
  L  A  E  A  D  N  U  O  P  E  P  K  O
E  N  F  L  M  C  A  R  T  W  H  E  E  L  C
D  I  L  G  B  R  E  A  D  C  O  R  N  S  R
E  O  Y  A  T  O  P  S  E  V  I  F  K  T  O
D  C  P  E  N  N  Y  N  I  L  S  C  T  I  W
I  O  R  E  I  G  T  R  I  Y  A  L  H  B  N
U  E  U  L  R  W  K  C  U  B  W  A  S  O  R
Q  E  O  B  O  E  O  T  N  O  F  F  S  W  E
  A  N  U  L  E  E  E  P  U  R  S  L  T
    L  O  F  O  E  D  I  N  A  R  O
      D  R  R  O  E  V  R  N  N
        G  K  I  N  B  L  C
```

Answers on page 30.

Look Up!

Every word listed below is contained within this group of letters. Words can be found horizontally, vertically, or diagonally. They may read either backward or forward.

```
                    S
                 A  P  S
              E  S  K  M  N
     Z  E  P  B  T  C  R  A  I  N  B  O  W
        S  N  A  I  C  L  K  L  L  F  L
           R  A  L  R  I  I  E  U  B
              O  L  T  D  S  P  O
              U  B  E  P  K  S  P  S  S
           D  S  B  T  Y  R  T  E  J  E  U
        S  T  E  N  A  L  P  I  Z  M  O  O  N
                 S  T  E  A  A
                 T  S  R
                    S
```

AIRPLANE	JET	SATELLITE
BATS	KITE	SKY
BIRDS	MARS	STAR
BLIMP	MOON	SUN
CLOUDS	PLANETS	UFO
ECLIPSE	RAINBOW	ZEPPELIN

Answers on page 30.

Painters

Every name listed below is contained within this group of letters. Names can be found horizontally, vertically, or diagonally. They may read either backward or forward.

```
D R D E K O O N I N G O Y A E
D E L A C R O I X W Y E T H L
B Y U E V Y D C R E P P O H P
O T E Q E I I E E G E L N M I
T T A L A N N E L R B L A O O
T C P R S R I C S E G H K T T
I O S I U I B U I S C L T R E
C R L T R E S N G U I O E E L
E R A K T E S E D U I T R L B
L E H G E U R B N G A T A O A
L G R G B E E U N N M G R M T
I G N I R A M F D A A I L I S
O I N N U I R F N H M Z O G N
T O S I O E S E C R Y D E R O
S T G S C T T T A S S A C C
```

BOTTICELLI	DA VINCI	HOLBEIN
BRAQUE	DEKOONING	HOPPER
BRUEGHEL	DELACROIX	KLEE
BUFFET	DUCHAMP	MANET
CASSATT	DURER	MARIN
CEZANNE	EL GRECO	MATISSE
CHAGALL	ERNST	MIRO
CONSTABLE	GAUGUIN	RYDER
COPLEY	GIOTTO	SEURAT
COROT	GOYA	SISLEY
CORREGGIO	GRIS	TURNER
COURBET	HALS	WYETH

Answers on page 30.

Double Talk

Every word listed below is contained within this group of letters. Words can be found horizontally, vertically, or diagonally. They may read either backward or forward.

```
O B L I G N I S G N I S A Z E
D O A E T O V E A L W Y I N A
O P B U N B A Y O G C R O H E
D R T O O N A C N A C O C Y M
V U S G O O I Z K I G A L L O
A O M E Y B E Y B A H O A P T
S W C D U M X I L C C B G K M
H H E R U P V L P P B K O O O
I L A U E M A Z I U G V P O T
L E M D T W E G H T A M A L K
N U E Y A E Y A O T O M P I I
U H L L W D B G U P N T A G D
L E L U D B Q A Y U A T I M K
I A O N U U U P I T L G E T I
W R P H E L I B A T N G O O D
```

ACK-ACK	DUM-DUM	POM-POM
AYE-AYE	GAGA	PUTT-PUTT
BONBON	GIGI	SING SING
BOO-BOO	GO-GO	SO-SO
BYE-BYE	HUBBA HUBBA	TA-TA
CANCAN	LULU	TOM-TOM
CHA-CHA	MAMA	TUTU
DADA	MUUMUU	WALLA WALLA
DIK-DIK	PAGO PAGO	YO-YO
DODO	PAPA	Answers on page 30.

Fruit Salad

Every word listed below is contained within this group of letters. Words can be found horizontally, vertically, or diagonally. They may read either backward or forward.

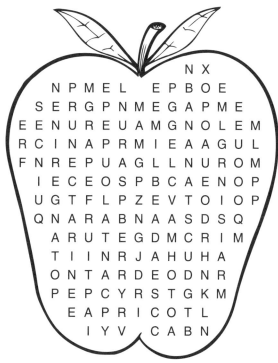

APPLE	GRAPEFRUIT	PEAR
APRICOT	GUAVA	PLUM
BANANA	LEMON	PRUNE
CANTALOUPE	LIME	QUINCE
CHERRY	MANGO	RAISIN
DAMSON	MELON	RASPBERRY
DATE	NECTARINE	SOURSOP
FIG	ORANGE	TANGERINE
GRAPE	PEACH	

Answers on page 31.

Fabrics

Terms in the grid are all types of fabric. Words can be found horizontally, vertically, or diagonally. They may read either backward or forward. The leftover letters spell a type of clothes not made of fabric.

ALPACA	DACRON	MUSLIN
BANLON	DENIM	NET
BROCADE	DUCK	ORGANDY
BURLAP	DUFFEL	PERCALE
CALICO	FELT	POPLIN
CAMBRIC	FLANNEL	RAYON
CANVAS	GABARDINE	SATIN
CASHMERE	GAUZE	SERGE
CHAMBRAY	GINGHAM	SILK
CHENILLE	HUCK	STAMMEL
CHIFFON	JERSEY	SUEDE
CHINO	LAMÉ	TRICOT
CORDUROY	LINEN	WOOL
COTTON	MADRAS	
CREPE	MOLESKIN	

HIDDEN MESSAGE: _____

_____

```
F  L  A  N  N  E  L  T  O  C  I  R  T  T  S
E  M  O  L  E  S  K  I  N  P  O  P  L  I  N
R  H  E  N  P  K  R  I  N  D  E  T  L  M  C
E  P  E  R  C  A  L  E  E  E  U  K  T  H  H
M  T  W  U  Y  S  C  N  B  N  N  F  A  O  E
H  P  H  O  U  E  I  A  R  R  I  M  F  J  N
S  M  N  M  O  D  N  G  O  K  B  T  S  E  I
A  A  B  U  R  L  A  P  C  R  C  E  A  R  L
C  D  V  A  O  U  E  H  A  A  R  U  O  S  L
R  R  B  N  Z  M  I  Y  D  G  L  S  D  E  E
N  A  C  E  A  F  M  F  E  L  T  I  A  Y  M
G  S  H  L  F  C  C  I  R  B  M  A  C  E  M
W  C  I  O  O  R  G  A  N  D  Y  L  R  O  A
G  I  N  G  H  A  M  S  U  E  D  E  O  O  T
T  C  O  R  D  U  R  O  Y  H  D  E  N  S  S
```

Answers on page 31.

Reciting Your ABCs

Every word listed below is contained within this group of letters. Words can be found diagonally. They may read either backward or forward.

```
        N T A T B M E G S A N
      D R E E O E X O S E A P R
    E S S U B I D A E W R E E I O
  N S S T B H A U E F E E E W T H S
  E A A Y I N T T Q W O B M E H L T
  H Y V N N D H R E E G R L O E I A
  V E E Y D E I T A N B C T E N E Z
  E W K O L R H A I A A H H W C E N
  O A W I F E A L S M E R O A O I Y
  Y B G H R T L D I U E B S R A D S
  T H M E Y E H N E V O P H T A Q T
  T A Y A P W O E L E I Y P R U E P
  R E O S L R O I T A N A O E U N C
  T E D L E E S R N I C I U K E L E
    T T A E Y W S R E G E R S O F
      L T A H E E Y Y U E E A L
        J P A H A A P B E R T
```

ARE WE THERE
YET?

AYE CAPTAIN

BEA ARTHUR

BOBBY VEE

CASPIAN SEA

EL CAMINO REAL

EWE LAMB

EYE OF THE
TIGER

GEE WHIZ

JAY SILVERHEELS

OH BE QUIET

OWE MONEY

QUEUE UP

SANDRA DEE

SEE THE LIGHT

SPELLING BEE

TEA FOR TWO

WHY WORRY

YOU SAID IT!

Answers on page 31.

Transportation

Words can be found horizontally, vertically, or diagonally. They may read either backward or forward. Leftover letters spell something to watch for.

```
            J E E P S
          A L T T L Y R
        U Y R A E A C K E
      N S O P V N H L Y L C
    T S L H T O A D O L C U A
  Y S L E C I R L N A A Y I S R
  L E T O A I P P A R U C H B D
  Y I U O O P D R R J P R R O R
  P P M T C E L I B O M O T U A
  E T S O L K A A T U U T H I Y
    K R S U G C D N G S O G E
      C O E S R A H E T M R
        A I A I A R R N R
          H K M N O S U
            N A D E S
```

AIRPLANE	HACK	SEDAN
AUTOMOBILE	HARDTOP	SHIP
BICYCLE	HOT ROD	SLED
BROUGHAM	JALOPY	STOCK CAR
BUS	JAUNTY	SULKY
CAR	JEEP	SURREY
CARRIAGE	LANDAU	TALLYHO
CHARIOT	LIMOUSINE	TROIKA
COACH	MOTORCYCLE	TROLLEY
COUPE	RACER	VAN
DRAY	SEAPLANE	

HIDDEN MESSAGE: _____

Answers on page 31.

S.F. Sts.

Terms in the grid all take their name from the same city. Words can be found horizontally, vertically, or diagonally. They may read either backward or forward. The leftover letters spell the name of an old TV show.

ASHBURY	HYDE	OAK
BAY	JACKSON	O'FARRELL
BUSH	JONES	POLK
CALIFORNIA	KEARNY	POST
CLAY	LAGUNA	POWELL
EDDY	LARKIN	PRADO
ELLIS	LEAVENWORTH	SANSOME
EMBARCADERO	LOMBARD	STOCKTON
FERN	MARKET	TAYLOR
FILLMORE	MASON	TURK
GEARY	MCALLISTER	VALLEJO
GOLDEN GATE	MISSION	VAN NESS
HAIGHT	MONTGOMERY	VEGA

HIDDEN MESSAGE: _____

_____

```
F I L L M O R E T H V E G A H
P R A D O T E D S L A G U N A
C N O S A M S Y T A N I O R K
E A K Y R U B H S A N R G E R
G O L D E N G A T E E S B H U
K O O I T S N O R D S U O Y T
R E P F F I F S A D S A D M N
O F A E K O Y C R H A D N C E
I F V R H T R O W N E V A E L
M C A N N A A N O T K C O T S
A L L R B Y E M I S S I O N E
R A L M R S G C J A C K S O N
K Y E Y R E M O G T N O M Y O
E A J M C A L L I S T E R A J
T P O S T S I L L E W O P B O
```

Answers on page 32.

Double Name Search

Every word listed below is contained within this group of letters, but there is a twist. Words can be found horizontally, vertically, or diagonally, but the two words of the clue will be parallel, like the circled example. They may read either backward or forward.

```
S K C A J Y T Y S P E T E X N T
A D R O L D M I Y R O S E S A N
L O I L L M V L D G E T I N L U
P R A E A A N R L R T V M O A F
A S I S D I L L O E A S H A L L
R F T N V O O N B D S W N C D T
W A I A G R N I E T R O O H I A
O L L N R O D A R E L D C H T R
O L J A C R E L G R N T S A R O
D E C O C O L D A A E J L Y M S
Y N O A H N Y M R N E E N I T
R T N T R N C B O R O R W E T R
N D R E R S N H E J G R I R A G
E A D E O N O Y U R E Y S N I I
D A L A L A N N T C R L D B E L
V N I A L D A H C E K Y B N O L
```

ADAM RICH	DARTH VADER	PETE ROSE
ALAN ALDA	HOWARD COSELL	RINGO STARR
ALAN FUNT	JACK LORD	RONALD REAGAN
ALAN LADD	JERRY LEWIS	RON ELY
ANDY GIBB	JOEL GREY	SALLY FIELD
BETTE DAVIS	JOHNNY CARSON	SAMMY DAVIS
CARROLL O'CONNOR	LINDA LAVIN	WOODY ALLEN
	LOIS LANE	
CHUCK BERRY	MARLON BRANDO	Answers on page 32.

I Hear a Snake!

Every word listed below is contained within this group of letters. Words can be found diagonally. They may read either backward or forward.

```
      T W S O W O G M G G R D E E
      X P R T A S I R L U E E K S
      L S E E A S D A A C E A I Y
    O S N A S L S I S R N S S S R S I N
    W H L S N S G S N E O S S A S N I C
    H P S E A G S G T L S W T S O S Y T
    D O R I E L I N U E E E S I K R O T
    R N G O I V E S N R R S T S O I I H
    S O A P C S E D S C T C S T S U R S
    N E P T S E O L E S E S S S S O W T
    C E O S S O S S E S E S S S T I R E
    R H A H G S S S S S R S S S E L C
    E P E R S S S S S E S E T S A T E T
    E R O S E S A E C E N S S S S L S L
    S F S R S R S C N I R T H A I P C P
      P E B S U E S T E V A I R D
      C O N S E U R A I S E E R C
      U T I V B T K D E W L R Y T
```

BRASS SECTION
BUSINESS SUIT
CHESS SET
CLASS STRUGGLE
CROSS SWORDS
DISTRESS SIGNAL
DRESS SHOES
FOR GOODNESS
  SAKE

GLASS SLIPPER
GRASS SKIRT
GUESS SO
MISS SAIGON
PASS SENTENCE
PRESS SECRETARY
PROCESS SERVER
ROSS SEA

SLEEVELESS
  SHIRT
STAINLESS STEEL
SUCCESS STORY
SWISS STEAK
WITNESS STAND

Answers on page 32.

What'll I Wear?

Terms in the grid are all related to clothing. Words can be found horizontally, vertically, or diagonally. They may read either backward or forward. The leftover letters spell a quote from Mark Twain.

ANORAK	DIRNDL	NYLONS
BERET	DRESS	PANTS
BIKINI	FEDORA	PARKA
BLAZER	FROCK	PONCHO
BLOUSE	GLOVES	SARONG
BOATER	HALTER	SHORTS
BONNET	JACKET	SLACKS
BRACES	JEANS	SNOOD
CAFTAN	JERSEY	STOLE
CLOAK	KIMONO	TIGHTS
CRAVAT	LIVERY	TOP HAT
DENIMS	MOTLEY	T-SHIRT
DICKEY	MUU-MUU	TUXEDO

HIDDEN MESSAGE: _____

_____

```
A B B I C O T R G D R E S S R
A N L L S N A E J T O P H A T
P B O N N E T T R E L O T S U
H A U R I B L A Z E R E N U X
K A S S A I S O A T B Y M S E
R K E E M K B B S U E U T N D
F R O C K I I T T S U H Y E O
C A F T A N N M R M A L C H L
P P S O A I T E O I O R C H E
A B G L H V J S D N H N O M T
N R L A A N A I S I O S O N I
T A O D L C C R B P R T T U G
S C V D T K K T C T L N O N H
S E E O E F E S T E H E D M T
A S S Y R F T N Y R E V I L S
```

Answers on page 32.

ANSWERS

TV Westerns (pages 2-3)

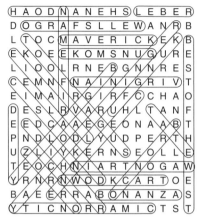

The leftover letters spell: Dan Blocker, Lorne Greene, Michael Landon, and Pernell Roberts.

Sandwich Stuff (page 5)

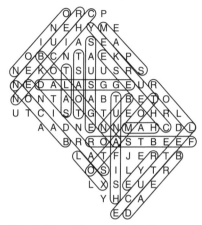

The leftover letters spell: Peanut butter and jelly.

British Universities (page 4)

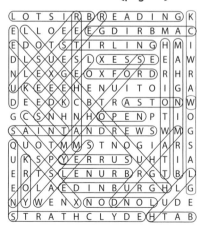

Body of Evidence (page 6)

Whatever the Weather (page 7)

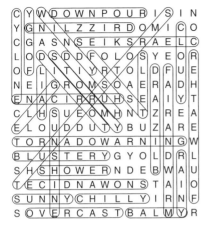

How About a Nice Bowl of Soup? (page 10)

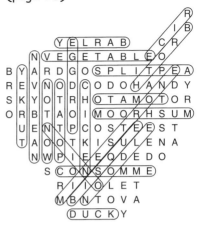

On the Mountaintop (pages 8-9)

Islands (page 11)

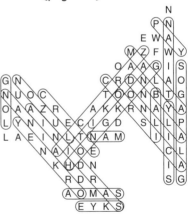

The leftover letters spell: Newfoundland.

Money, Money, Money (pages 12-13)

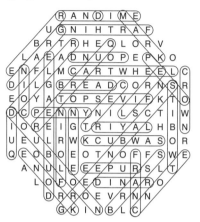

The leftover letters spell: The love of money is the root of all evil.

Look Up! (page 14)

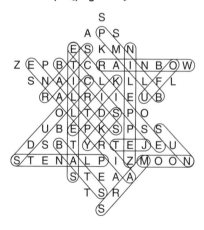

Painters (page 15)

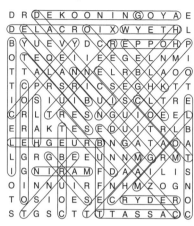

Double Talk (page 16)

Fruit Salad (page 17)

Reciting Your ABCs (page 20)

Fabrics (pages 18-19)

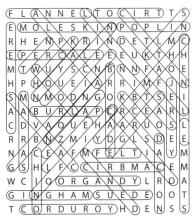

The leftover letters spell: The emperor's new clothes.

Transportation (page 21)

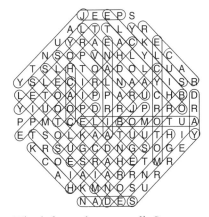

The leftover letters spell: Stop signs.

S.F. Sts. (pages 22-23)

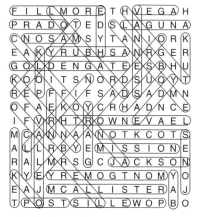

The leftover letters spell: The Streets of San Francisco.

I Hear a Snake! (page 25)

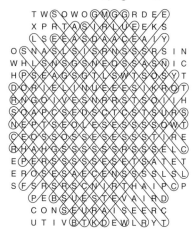

Double Name Search (page 24)

What'll I Wear? (pages 26-27)

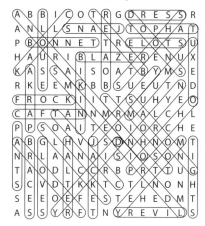

The leftover letters spell: Biographies are but the clothes and buttons of the man.